Journey Through History

The Greek
and Roman Eras

Translation: Jean Grasso Fitzpatrick

English translation © Copyright 1988 by Barron's Educational Series, Inc.

© Parramón Ediciones, S.A.
First Edition, February 1988
The title of the Spanish edition is *La edad antigua*

All inquiries should be addressed to:
Barron's Educational Series, Inc.
250 Wireless Boulevard
Hauppauge, New York 11788

Library of Congress Catalog Card No. 88-10382
International Standard Book No. 0-8120-3388-4
Library of Congress Cataloging-in-Publication Data

Vergés, Gloria.
  [Edad antigua. English]
  The Greek and Roman eras / [illustrated by] Carme Peris ; [written by]
Gloria & Oriol Vergés ; [translation, Jean Grasso Fitzpatrick]. — 1st ed.
    p. cm. — (Journey through history)
  Translation of: Edad antigua.
  Summary: An illustrated history of the Greek and Roman eras, with a
fictional story involving children to depict the time in history.
  ISBN 0-8120-3388-4
  1. History, Ancient—Juvenile literature. [1. Greece—History—To
142 B.C. 2. Rome—History. 3. History, Ancient.] I. Peris, Carme, ill.
II. Vergés, Oriol. III. Title. IV. Series: Vergés, Gloria. Viaje a través de la
historia. English.
D57.V4713 1988
938—dc19   88-10382
                                                                     CIP
Printed in Spain by Sirven Grafic   AC
Gran Vía, 754 Barcelona
Legal Deposit: B-19.608-88

890   987654321

Journey Through History

The Greek
and Roman Eras

Carme Peris
Glòria & Oriol Vergés

CHILDRENS PRESS CHOICE
A Barron's title selected for educational distribution
ISBN 0-516-08472-0

The *polis*—as the ancient Greek city of Athens was called—was a lively place. In the *agora*, or main square, the whole population would gather to begin the procession to the Acropolis—the city's highest point, where all the most important temples were.

"The agora was a lot more crowded yesterday than today," said Dimitri.

"That's because the politician who's running for governor of Athens was making a speech," answered his friend. "He spoke very well! I didn't understand much of what he had to say, but my father said that if he's elected, it would be good for business—so we'll all get richer."

"I'm going with my friends," said Diana. "We have to bring the veil of the goddess, Athena. I've come straight from the temple, and the procession is already starting."

The Greek gods and goddesses looked just like ordinary men and women. Each of them was supposed to watch over one activity or task, and they were believed to be immortal.

"Homer is the best potter in the whole city!" said Dimitri.

"That's for sure!" agreed Panos. "What beautiful jars and vases! I've counted them, and I think there are fifteen different kinds."

"What I like best are the drawings and designs," said Diana. "That must have been a lot of work, sir. Wasn't it?"

"It certainly was," answered the potter, with a sigh. "I made these jars for a ship that's leaving tomorrow for Sicily to get olive oil. And I'm selling those urns back there—see them?—to a colony overseas. And my customers are always in a terrible rush!"

People of today can still see beautiful ancient Greek jars in museums. They can also visit the remains of ancient cities all around the Mediterranean Sea—like this one on the peninsula where modern Spain is located. These cities were inhabited by Greeks who traded peacefully with the people of nearby towns. The people were amazed at the goods brought by the ships coming from Athens.

"The Greeks called this city Emporium," explains Mother.
"What does Emporium mean?" asks Justin.
"Commercial center," she replies. "They came here and sold fine earthenware and colored fabrics—products that the people of these lands didn't know how to make."

In return, the Greeks received precious metals. In time, the Greeks taught the colonists how to make coins, which helped encourage commerce among them.

"Learning how to read and write isn't too hard," said Dimitri. "Anyway, we need to learn so that we'll be able to run our businesses."

"Well, that's true for you because you want to be a merchant like the rest of our family!" replied Panos. "But I'm planning to devote my life to politics, like my father."

"What I really like is the gymnasium!" said Kyriakos. "Yesterday I did a high jump, and our Spartan gym teacher congratulated me."

Greek boys—just like children of today—went to school to learn reading, writing, and arithmetic, and to develop healthy bodies. Their teachers were usually Greeks or people who came from the colonies. A few were slaves.

Women did not participate in public life and were hardly seen in the street. Little girls didn't even go to school!

"Poor man! How he must be suffering!" exclaimed the doctor.

Greek physicians were highly skilled. First they would clean a wound well, and then they would dull the pain with ointments that they prepared themselves. The most celebrated doctors were those who cured the most wounded soldiers.

Asclepius was the god of medical arts, and he was said to protect both patients and doctors. In ancient Greece, Hippocrates was the most popular and highly respected physician. His followers were required to take an oath promising to place care for the sick above all other obligations. Today, doctors the world over still take the very same oath!

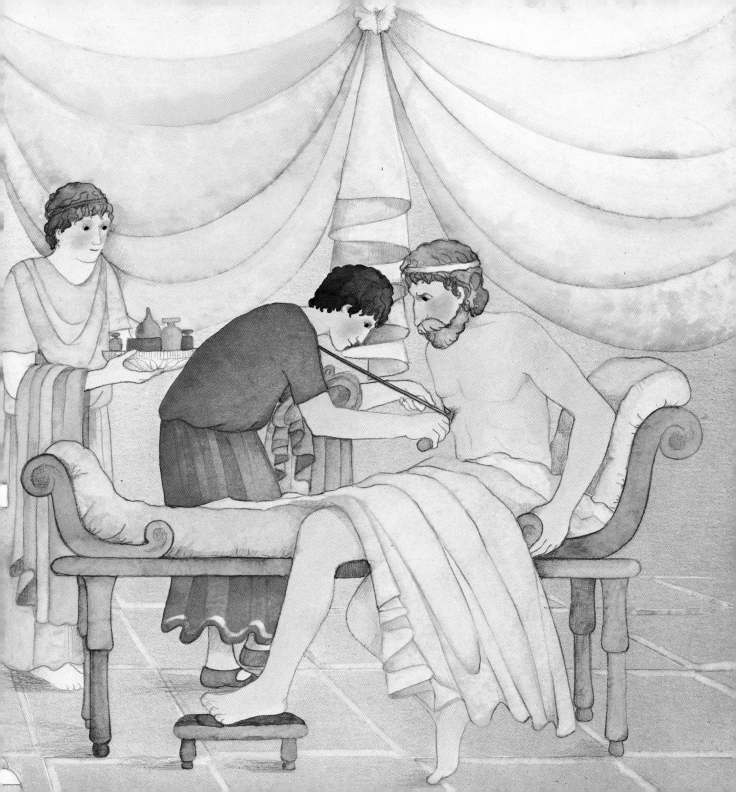

Greek athletic competitions took place at the gymnasium. Every four years, huge crowds of citizens and athletes met to celebrate the Olympic Games and have music and poetry contests. The athletes participated for the sake of competition, not to win money. The Greeks believed that the ideal human had a healthy mind in a healthy body. To express their admiration for the Olympic athletes, they put up sculptures of them everywhere.

"What a great run!" cried Dimitri. "What a smooth stride!" Panos agreed. "And he never breaks his rhythm! He'll win for sure!"

The Greeks were the first to write plays, which were presented on a stage at the bottom of a small hill. The audience sat on the slope of the hill. In the tragedies, the heroes suffered countless misfortunes by the will of the gods. In the comedies, all sorts of funny things happened to make the audience laugh.

"I really like the theater, but the masks scare me a little bit," said Kyriakos.

"I like the comedies," replied Diana. "Did you realize that if the actors didn't wear these masks—which serve as sounding boxes to make their voices louder we wouldn't be able to hear the beautiful lines they were saying?"

"Roman soldiers are the greatest in the world!" exclaimed Flavius. "Look how proud the victorious general is! He has led his legions to conquer new lands for Rome."

"And see how many slaves they bring!" replied Lydia. "My father would like to buy some, so that they can work our fields. Imagine—seven carriages filled with captured jewelry and treasures are being driven under the arch of triumph!"

The well-disciplined Roman legions conquered the whole known world for the glory of the Roman Empire.

Some of the conquered people were taken as slaves. The other inhabitants of the conquered lands remained under Roman rule. Little by little, they learned the language, customs, and way of life of their conquerors. Over the years, Roman culture was carried to many of the countries of Europe and northern Africa.

"Hurry up and fix my hair," a Roman citizen ordered her slave. "I have to go to the Forum!"

"Mother, may we go with you to the square?" asked her son.

"Yes, let us come!" begged her daughter. "There's going to be an auction of slaves who have just been brought in from very far-off lands."

Wealthy Romans lived in houses that were comfortable and pleasant. The slaves did tasks that are done today by machine. Some Romans treated their slaves kindly, but slaves could not leave their masters or enjoy freedom.

In addition, the children of slaves were born into slavery.

"What is this senator talking about?"

"I'm not sure because I just got here, but everyone's listening to him very carefully," answered Lydia. "I think he wants a new law passed in the Senate."

The Roman senators passed laws that affected the daily life of the citizens. The Senate met in the Capitol just as our Senate does today.

Both the senators and distinguished citizens covered themselves with *togas*, long, wide garments that they wore over their short tunics. The senators had to be good speakers in order to win debates and be respected by the citizens.

The Roman circus was oval in shape. Circus performances featured four-horse chariot races and battles between slave-warriors called *gladiators*.

"I've never seen so many people before!" said one spectator. "It's exciting to see the charioteer standing in his chariot and holding four horses by the reins!" said another. "I like the chariots a lot better than the gladiators. In gladiator bouts one contestant always dies."

Chariot races and wrestling were very popular among the Romans. During spectacles that lasted longer than a day, the emperors even distributed food among the spectators. The circus took the minds of the people off their poverty. Because of the excitement of the spectacles, they were more willing to live with their many problems.

The Romans were great architects. They put up beautiful buildings and monuments and constructed highways. They also built *aqueducts* for carrying water to the cities. Sometimes bridges—with one or two rows of arches—carried the aqueduct instead of a roadway. These constructions—some of which are still preserved today—greatly impressed people living under Roman rule.

"Have you seen this bridge?" asked Lydia. "It's perfect! I'm sure it will last forever!"

"What I want to do is lift one of these stone blocks," said Flavius.

"Why?"

"I made a bet with Claudius, and he's pretty strong. But I don't know.... Somehow, I don't think I'm going to be able to lift this stone."

Standing before the ruins of a splendid past, modern children listen quietly to their parents' explanations.

"The volcano, Vesuvius, erupted on these beautiful cities, Pompeii and Herculaneum, and they were buried," says their mother. "The lava flew out of the volcano and covered the houses, the stores and the streets so quickly that it hardly destroyed anything. As a result, archeologists have been able to dig out cities that are nearly intact, with paintings on the walls of the houses, and the furniture still in the bedrooms."

"But did everyone die?" asks the boy.

"Yes, unfortunately. And now, in reconstructing the Roman way of life, we have grown to understand that it was very similar to our own."

A GUIDE FOR PARENTS AND TEACHERS

The Polis and Agoras

In classical Greece, the cities or *polis* were independent from one another. The *agora*, or main square, was the central meeting place of the citizens. The Acropolis was the walled area where temples were erected. The Greek gods were depicted to look like people. The Greeks believed that the gods lived on Mount Olympus and that they were immortal.

Greek Pottery

It was characterized by its variety of form—casks, jars, urns—and by its decoration—ochre figures on a black background or dark figures on a light background. The pottery was both useful and beautiful. It was frequently exported to other Mediterranean towns.

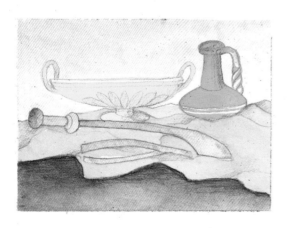

Science in Greece

The Greek philosophers were very much like today's scientists. They tried to give a rational explanation to natural phenomena and the behavior of human beings. They especially distinguished themselves in geometry and medicine; the latter was based on natural cures and on great respect for the patient. In education, they emphasized harmony between body and mind.

The Olympics

These were festivals during which the inhabitants of different cities competed against one another. They were celebrated every four years. These competitions and sporting events were revived at the end of the nineteenth century on the initiative of Pierre de Coubertin, in the same spirit of brother- and sisterhood among nations through sport.

The Greek Theater

Another Greek innovation that was passed on to posterity is the theater. Tragedy presented the suffering of human beings because of destiny and the will of the gods. Comedy, on the other hand, which made fun of vices and customs, provides us with evidence of everyday life.

The Roman Army

The Romans inherited a large part of the Greek cultural legacy, although they gave it an imperialistic tone. There were great social inequalities in Roman society, and slavery (as in Greece) was permitted by law. The army played an important role in the expansion of the Roman Empire, which spread over the Mediterranean and large parts of Europe, Asia, and Africa.

Romanization

If the Greeks discovered politics, the Romans developed government, with precise laws and efficient organization. The Roman language and civilization were carried to all corners of the Empire. This process is known as Romanization. One of its most important consequences was to give a common root, Latin, to many of the European languages that are spoken today.

Roman Art and Spectacle

Great popular spectacles were frequent in Rome. In the imperial age they served as a way for the emperors to demonstrate their power and helped keep down popular discontent. They took place in the Coliseum, which, along with the aqueducts, the arches and the bridges, is one of the best-known Roman monuments. Roman art was designed for practical use. Many of these works have been preserved to this day.

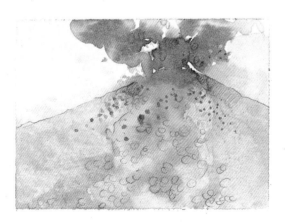

The City of Pompeii

Thanks to the lava of Vesuvius that covered it, the structure of Pompeii has been preserved until our time. For this reason we are able to know the pattern of daily life of a Roman city, its houses, its shops. Silhouettes of dogs and people who were unable to escape the volcanic eruption and were trapped by the lava have also been discovered.